Scripture-Based Answers to Some
GOSPEL WHYS

by

Kelly G. Jones

PUBLISHING CO
EST. 1920
PITTSBURGH, PENNSYLVANIA 15238

The contents of this work, including, but not limited to, the accuracy of events, people, and places depicted; opinions expressed; permission to use previously published materials included; and any advice given or actions advocated are solely the responsibility of the author, who assumes all liability for said work and indemnifies the publisher against any claims stemming from publication of the work.

All Rights Reserved
Copyright © 2021 by Kelly G. Jones

No part of this book may be reproduced or transmitted, downloaded, distributed, reverse engineered, or stored in or introduced into any information storage and retrieval system, in any form or by any means, including photocopying and recording, whether electronic or mechanical, now known or hereinafter invented without permission in writing from the publisher.

Dorrance Publishing Co
585 Alpha Drive
Pittsburgh, PA 15238
Visit our website at *www.dorrancebookstore.com*

ISBN: 978-1-6491-3750-0
eISBN: 978-1-6491-3941-2

This material is neither made, provided, approved, nor endorsed by Intellectual Reserve, Inc. or The Church of Jesus Christ of Latter-day Saints. Any content or opinions expressed, implied or included in or with the material are solely those of the owner and not those Intellectual Reserve, Inc. or The Church of Jesus Christ of Latter-day Saints.

Tablet of Contents

About the Author vii

Foreword ix

Chapter 1: Why Organized Religion? 1

Chapter 2: Why Faith? 5

Chapter 3: Why Repent? 11

Chapter 4: Why Make and Keep Covenants? 17

Chapter 5: Why Temples? 21

Chapter 6: Why Prayer? 25

Chapter 7: Why Sabbath Day Observance? 29

Chapter 8: Why Perfection? (Can I be perfect?) 33

Afterword: My Testimony 35

About the Author

Kelly G. Jones is a wife and mother of six children. She is also part owner of a family-based guardrail installation company that she has run from her home since 1995. Kelly has filled many callings in The Church of Jesus Christ of Latter-day Saints over the years, including Relief Society President, Cub Scout leader, and Seminary teacher. She has a love of the scriptures and loves to study how the different books of scripture interact and support one another. By studying and connecting information from all available scriptures and other sources, she has gained a deeper understanding of Gospel topics.

Foreword

When I taught seminary for five years, I gained an appreciation for the depth of knowledge that can be obtained by a thorough study of the scriptures. The scriptures are like an onion. The surface read gives a good story. Read deeper and there is a moral to the story to apply to our lives. Read and cross-reference with associated scriptures and a broader picture of what is being taught can enrich our knowledge. Study by topic using all available sources, and things come to light you never thought of before. Connections can be made between topics that weren't obvious with the first several readings. It will take a lifetime and beyond to understand all there is to gain from simple and more complex scripture study.

I wish I knew as a teenager or even a twenty-ager what I learned and started to apply as a seminary teacher. Just think of how much further ahead in my knowledge I could be now! My hope is that this book will start you on a journey of gaining knowledge (and applying it) so that you can have a strong knowledge of what this life is all about. God has given us the textbook and more. But He will not spoon-feed us the information we need. We have to find a desire to know and a will to work at knowing.

I have attempted to use the scriptures to answer some of the basic gospel questions that I have answered over and over in classes I have taught. For those unfamiliar with the books I reference, here is a list:

- The Holy Bible – Authorized King James Version with explanatory notes and cross-references to the standard works of The Church of Jesus Christ of Latter-day Saints. (No notes after reference)
- The Topical Guide that is published with the Bible listed above.
- The Bible Dictionary that is published with the Bible listed above.
- The Book of Mormon Another Testament of Jesus Christ (BM after reference)
- The Doctrine and Covenants of The Church of Jesus Christ of Latter-day Saints (D&C)

- The Pearl of Great Price – A selection from the Revelations and translations, and narrations of Joseph Smith. (PGP after reference)

If I can answer even one person's inquiry with this text, then I will consider the effort worth it. May this be a springboard for your desire to learn more.

CHAPTER 1

Why Organized Religion?

"Behold, mine house is a house of order, saith the Lord God, and not a house of confusion," (Doctrine and Covenants 132:8) and since God and Christ are "...the same yesterday, and today, and forever" (Hebrews 13:8) then we can look to ancient text to see how His house is organized.

Moses wrote the first five books of the bible. He was the first prophet to record how the organization worked. Moses led about a million people out of Egypt, cross-country, with him as the sole leader and judge. His father-in-law was the priest of Middian and could see the stress this caused Moses, so he advised him how to organize his people:

> "...thou shalt teach them ordinances and laws, and shalt shew them the way wherein they must walk, and the work that they must do. Moreover thou shalt provide out of all the people able men, such as fear God, men of truth, hating covetousness; and place such over them, to be rulers of thousands, and rulers of hundreds, rulers of fifties, and rulers of tens: And let them judge the people at all seasons: and it shall be, that every great matter they shall bring unto thee, but every small matter they shall judge: so shall it be easier for thyself, and they shall bear the burden with thee. If thou shalt do this thing, and God command thee so, then thou shalt be able to endure..." (Exodus 18:20-23)

Moses followed this advice, and by Exodus 24 Moses, with three others and seventy of the elders of Israel, went up (assuming on the mountain), and saw the God of Israel, and described Him. (Exodus 24:9-10) He must have found some very righteous men "such as fear God, men of truth, [and] hating covetousness" (Exodus 18:21) to be the leaders of the organization he had in the wilderness for them to see God.

Note that God the Father and the Lord, Jesus Christ, were directing all these actions. Jethro in the quote above said, "...and God command thee so." Later, before his death, Moses was directed by the Lord to take Joshua before the priest and by the laying on of hands "gave him a charge." (Numbers 27:18-23) This put Joshua in charge of leading the people. Priests had authority to speak for God and give messages from Him to leaders and the people. They also laid their hands on people to anoint them kings or to ordain them to priesthood offices. So God, through priests, chose leaders, prophets, and priests to establish and continue the priesthood organization.

This priesthood had an order to it. In Psalms it states, "Thou art a priest for ever after the order of Melchizedek." (Psalms 110:4) Melchizedek was the king of Salem and "was the priest of the most high God." (Gen 14:18) About 550 years before Christ, The Book of Mormon Another Testament of Christ records a similar organization on the American continent; "I, Jacob, having been called of God, and ordained after the manner of his holy order..." (2 Nephi 6:2, BM) About four hundred years later, a man named "Alma, having authority from God, ordained priests." (Mosiah 18:18, BM) Though these two civilizations had an ocean between them, they had the same priesthood organization.

Moving on to the New Testament, Christ gave Peter the "keys of the kingdom of heaven" explaining that "...whatsoever thou shalt bind on earth shall be bound in heaven; and whatsoever thou shalt loose on earth shall be loosed in heaven." (Matthew 16:19) He called twelve apostles in Luke 6:13, and seventy to help teach in Luke 10:1. They in turn ordained elders (Acts 14:23). The apostles and elders met together to make decisions for the churches/congregations they had established throughout the country. (Acts 15:6) In his letter to the Ephesians, Paul described the church as "...fellow citizens with the saints, and of the household of God; and are built upon the foundation of the apostle and prophets, Jesus Christ himself being the chief cornerstone." (Ephesians 2:19-20) In other epistles, Paul mentions bishops and deacons, (Philippians 1:1) and reminded Titus to "ordain elders in every city." (Titus 1:5)

God's house is a house of order. He has given this order through the priesthood of God. On May 15, 1829 John the Baptist (a resurrected being), "acting under the direction of Peter, James, and John, the ancient Apostles, who held the keys of the higher priesthood, which was called the Priesthood of Melchizedek" (Doctrine and Covenants Section 13, heading), conferred upon Joseph Smith and Oliver Cowdery the Aaronic Priesthood, the same priesthood Aaron had in the wilderness with Moses. Joseph Smith was later ordained and confirmed an apostle by the hands of Peter, James, and John. (Doctrine and Covenants 27:12) Joseph and Oliver were told at that time to "lift up your hearts and rejoice, for unto you the kingdom, or in other words, the keys of the church have been given." (Doctrine and Covenants 42:69) The same keys that Peter, James, and John used to set up the church in their day as recorded in the New Testament.

With the keys and the priesthood on the earth again, organizing and moving forward the Kingdom of God in an orderly fashion as directed, wouldn't it be prudent to couple ourselves to the organization that has the authority to move God's work forward? We must remember, "…unto every kingdom is given a law; and unto every law there are certain bounds also and conditions. All beings who abide not in those conditions are not justified." (Doctrine and Covenants 88:38-39) In order to "abide" these conditions we must know what they are. We must be educated, informed, and willing to submit to God's conditions to reap the rewards God offers. Organized religion is to help us systematically learn those conditions and to help us meet the conditions. Organized religion is also to maintain records on earth so that the things that are "[bound] on earth shall be bound in heaven." (Matt 16:19)

CHAPTER 2

Why Faith?

Many things in life require faith. When we plant seeds in the ground, we have faith that the sun will rise and the weather will cooperate enough to let that seed grow. When we see highway signs, or warning signs, we act in faith that the person(s) that put that sign up knew what they were talking about. We don't have to know how everything works before we turn it on to take advantage of the benefits of our modern devices (electronics, cars, phones, electricity, televisions, etc.), we simply have to have faith that the manufacturers did their job properly.

"Faith is a principle of action and power that motivates our day-to-day activities. Would we study and learn if we did not believe we could obtain wisdom and knowledge? Would we work each day if we did not hope that by doing so, we could accomplish something? Would a farmer plant if he did not expect to harvest? Each day we act upon things we hope for when we cannot see the end result." (Gospel Principles, pg. 101)

To implement faith, it takes action on our part. We have to actually plant the seed, flip the switch, take the exit, or turn on the ignition. Faith in God and Jesus Christ is no different because in order to implement faith, it takes action on our part. We have to pray, obey the commandments, pay our tithing, or follow the impressions we get from the Holy Ghost (sometimes recognized as a "gut feeling," or an "instinct"). Only after action can we see the fruits of our labors. Some fruits will come fairly quickly while others will take time.

The prophet Ether describes faith as "...things which are hoped for and not seen; wherefore, dispute not because ye see not, for ye receive no witness until after the trial of your faith." (Ether 12:6, BM) The actions we take prove we have faith. Continuing those actions until we see the results is the trial of our faith.

So the question is, "Why would God want us to act with faith?" The answer is, "Because this life is a test." God wants us to see how we will use our agency when presented with decisions, problems, or trials. He wants us to see what we are made of. Are we persistent enough to finish something even when it is hard? Will we follow guidance and commandments without always knowing the whys?

In the Sermon on the Mount Jesus explained "…your heavenly Father knoweth that ye have need of all these things. But seek ye first the kingdom of God and his righteousness; and all these things shall be added unto you." (Matt 6:32-33) Do we trust Him? Do we really have faith that He is there and that He meant what he said to Moses:

"…this is my work and my glory – to bring to pass the immortality and eternal life of man." (Moses 1:39, PGP)

If we can't answer yes to those questions, then we have our starting point. Does God exist? How can we get a knowledge of that basic principle? FAITH. We start with the faith-filled assumption that this is true. God does exist. Then we act on it. How? Pray, keep the commandments, read the scriptures, serve one another. Do these basics for long enough to see the results. "… By their fruits ye shall know them." (Matt 7:20) How do these actions make you feel? How have they changed your life? Do you see enough fruit to move forward to the next step?

You can, through your own actions, test every commandment or piece of advice God has given us. Just like anything else you want to learn about, you have to put in the time to study what those commandments and pieces of advice are. Start with the scriptures. Then, when you realize the scriptures are records of prophets of God that took the time to write these things down for the rest of humanity, you can turn to the prophets and apostles of our day to read and hear their words.

About 600 years before Christ was born, Nephi was looking for knowledge and "…was desirous also that I might see, and hear, and know of these things, by the power of the Holy Ghost, which is the gift of God unto all those who diligently seek him, as well in times of old as in the time that he should manifest himself unto the children of men. For he is the same yesterday, today, and forever; and the way is prepared for all men from the foundation of the world, if it so be that they repent and come unto him. For he that diligently seeketh shall find; and the mysteries of God shall be unfolded unto them, by the power of the Holy Ghost, as well in these times as in times of old, and as well in times of old as in times to come;" (1 Nephi 10: 17-19, BM)

The "power of the Holy Ghost" is there for us to tap into. We need to learn how to recognize its influence in our lives. Once when my first two children were young, they were sleeping on bunk beds. My oldest was three or four and was on the top bunk. I was tucking them in and he was quite bouncy. The spirit told me to move to the end of the metal framed bunk bed. I did and my son bounced up to the pillow and accidentally bounced into a somersault. I had moved to the right position just in time to catch his bottom so the middle of his back would not come down on the metal frame.

Another time, when my last two children were in high school, we were returning from a visit to my parents. While traveling north of Jackson Hole, Wyoming the spirit told me to "watch the oncoming traffic like a hawk." I was coming into a blind corner and a row of cars was coming toward me. As I rounded the corner the last car in the line was completely in my lane. I hit the brakes and took two wheels off the road, heading straight for the end of a run of guardrail. The other car's driver "woke up" and pulled back into his lane just in time for me to come back onto the road and miss the guardrail. If I had been at all distracted, we would have hit head-on. I was very thankful the spirit gave me the heads-up.

It takes practice to recognize when the spirit speaks. It sometimes feels like an instinct or gut feeling. It will almost always be a direct thought to take action, "do this," "go here," "turn here," "take that with you," "don't do …," etc. As we learn to listen to those thoughts and act on them, they can become stronger and more direct. Sometimes, when we ignore those thoughts, we regret not acting on them. Those are the times we are learning.

My husband says he is thankful for the times he didn't listen and suffered the consequences, because those times taught him what to listen for. When something really important came up, he was paying attention and it saved our son's life.

Since God does not change, we can have faith that He gives us the same opportunities presented to others throughout the scriptures. He expects us to learn, listen, and test those things so we can know for ourselves what is true. He has never expected blind obedience. President Spencer W. Kimball taught:

> "Often we hear: 'Nobody can tell me what clothes to wear, what I shall eat or drink. No one can outline my Sabbaths, appropriate my earnings, nor in any way limit my personal freedoms! I do as I please! I give no blind obedience!'"
>
> Blind obedience! How little they understand!…

When men obey commands of a creator, it is not blind obedience. How different is the cowering of a subject to his totalitarian monarch and the dignified, willing obedience one gives to his God? The dictator is ambitious, selfish, and has ulterior motives. God's every command is righteous, every directive purposeful, and all for the good of the governed. The first may be blind obedience, but the latter is certainly faith obedience. ...

Is it blind obedience when one regards the sign "High Voltage—Keep Away" or is it the obedience of faith in the judgment of experts who know the hazard?

Is it blind obedience when the air traveler fastens his seat belt as that sign flashes or is it confidence in the experience and wisdom of those who know more of hazards and dangers?

Is it blind obedience when the little child gleefully jumps from the table into the strong arms of its smiling father, or is this implicit trust in a loving parent who feels sure of his catch and who loves the child better than life itself? ...

Is it then blind obedience when we, with our limited vision, elementary knowledge, selfish desires, ulterior motives, and carnal urges, accept and follow the guidance and obey the commands of our loving Father who ... created a world for us, loves us, and has planned a constructive program for us, wholly without ulterior motive, whose greatest joy and glory is to "bring to pass the immortality and eternal life" of all his children? [See Moses 1:39. PGP]8

It is not blind obedience, even without total understanding, to follow a Father who has proved himself." (Teachings of the Presidents of the Church Spencer W. Kimball, pg. 139-140)

Faith is imperative. "...if there be no faith among the children of men, God can do no miracle among them;" (Ether 12:12) "... (I)t is by faith that miracles are wrought; and it is by faith that angels appear and minister unto men; wherefore, if these things have ceased wo be unto the children of men, for it is because of unbelief and all is vain." (Moroni 7:37, BM)

It was by faith that Moses parted the red sea (Hebrews 11:7), Daniel came out of the lion's den unharmed (Dan 6:16-22), the three young men came out of the fiery furnace unharmed (Daniel 3:17-27), Alma and Amulek caused the prison walls to fall (Alma 14: 26-29, BM), the list goes on. It was by faith that Joseph Smith, at fourteen years of age, went into the woods to pray for answers and was visited by God the Father and Jesus Christ. (Joseph Smith History, PGP) We, too, can gain the faith needed to go through the tests and trials of our mortal lives and beyond.

God cares. He is our Father. He wants us to learn and grow. He has given us a lot of helps to guide us through this life. We have to simply have faith enough to act so we can learn for ourselves right from wrong and find the truths available to us.

CHAPTER 3

Why Repent?

Before we can understand why we must repent, we have to understand what repentance really is. Theodore M. Burton, as a general authority of The Church of Jesus Christ of Latter-day Saints, referred to times when;

> "...a bishop will write, 'I feel he has suffered enough!' But suffering is not repentance. Suffering comes from lack of complete repentance. A stake president will write, 'I feel he has been punished enough!' But punishment is not repentance. Punishment follows disobedience and precedes repentance. A husband will write, 'My wife has confessed everything!' But confession is not repentance. Confession is an admission of guilt that occurs as repentance begins. A wife will write, 'My husband is filled with remorse!' But remorse is not repentance. Remorse and sorrow continue because a person has not yet fully repented. Suffering, punishment, confession, remorse, and sorrow may sometimes accompany repentance, but they are not repentance. What, then, is repentance?" (August 1988 Ensign, "The Meaning of Repentance")

He goes on to explain the origins of the word 'repentance':

> "The Old Testament was originally written in Hebrew, and the word used in it to refer to the concept of repentance is shube. We can better understand what shube means by

reading a passage from Ezekiel and inserting the word shube, along with its English translation. To the "watchmen" appointed to warn Israel, the Lord says:

"When I say unto the wicked, O wicked man, thou shalt surely die; if thou dost not speak to warn the wicked from his way, that wicked man shall die in his iniquity; but his blood will I require at thine hand.

"Nevertheless, if thou warn the wicked of his way to turn from [shube] it; if he do not turn from [shube] his way, he shall die in his iniquity; but thou hast delivered thy soul. ...

"Say unto them, as I live, saith the Lord God, I have no pleasure in the death of the wicked; but that the wicked turn from [shube] his way and live." (Ezek. 33:8–11.)

I know of no kinder, sweeter passage in the Old Testament than those beautiful lines. In reading them, can you think of a kind, wise, gentle, loving Father in Heaven pleading with you to shube, or turn back to him—to leave unhappiness, sorrow, regret, and despair behind and turn back to your Father's family, where you can find happiness, joy, and acceptance among his other children?" (August 1988 Ensign, "The Meaning of Repentance")

The New Testament was originally written in Greek and teaches a similar concept when we go to the original Greek meaning of the word used in its text that was translated into the word repentance in our English version.

"When Jesus said 'repent,' His disciples recorded that command in the Greek language with the verb metanoeo. This powerful word has great significance. In this word, the prefix meta means 'change.' The suffix relates to four important Greek terms: nous, meaning 'the mind'; gnosis, meaning 'knowledge'; pneuma, meaning 'spirit'; and pnoe, meaning 'breath.' Thus, when Jesus said 'repent' He asked us to change—to change our mind, knowledge, and spirit—even our breath." ("Repentance and Conversion," Ensign or Liahona, May 2007, 103)

Thus, to repent, we change our thinking to the point of changing our actions so we can BECOME whom we are capable of becoming.

Now we can explore the "Why" we need to repent. Let's start with remembering who we are. Where did we come from? Jeremiah a prophet from the Old Testament was told by the Lord;

"Before I formed thee in the belly, I knew thee; and before thou camest forth out of the womb I sanctified thee, and I ordained thee a prophet unto the nations." (Jer 1:5)

Abraham, also of Old Testament times, was shown the pre-earth life and "...the intelligences that were organized before the world was; and among all these there were many of the noble and great ones." Then the Lord told Abraham, "thou are one of them; thou wast chosen before thou wast born." (Abraham 3:22-23, PGP)

God knew us before we were born. Some of us (probably more than we think) were noble and great ones! Imagine, if you were even close to one of the noble and great ones in your pre-earth life and didn't do as well down here because you thought "it is too hard to change," how will you feel for the rest of eternity when you can remember your pre-earth life, and your potential, and know you didn't follow through with your dreams of success?

In 1918, President Joseph F. Smith, President of the Church of Jesus Christ of Latter-day Saints, was shown how Christ organized missionary work among the spirits of those that had once lived on the earth (D&C section 138). During this vision he saw the Prophet Joseph Smith, Hyrum Smith (Joseph F. Smith's father), Brigham Young, John Taylor, Wilford Woodruff, and others that had already passed on, and was shown that:

> "...they were also among the noble and great ones who were chosen in the beginning to be rulers in the Church of God. Even before they were born, they, with many others, received their first lessons in the world of spirits and were prepared to come forth in the due time of the Lord to labor in his vineyard for the salvation of the souls of men." (D&C 138:53-55)

In about 82 BC Alma was teaching how men were called and ordained priests. He used terms like "foundation of the world," and "the first place" to denote the pre-earth life. He taught that these priests were ordained:

> "...being called and prepared from the foundation of the world according to the foreknowledge of God, on account of their exceeding faith and good works; in the first place being

> left to choose good or evil; therefore they having chosen good, and exercising exceedingly great faith, are called with a holy calling, yea, with that holy calling which was prepared with, and according to, a preparatory redemption for such. And thus they have been called to this holy calling on account of their faith, while others would reject the Spirit of God on account of the hardness of their hearts and blindness of their minds, while, if it had not been for this they might have had as great privilege as their brethren. Or in fine, in the first place they were on the same standing with their brethren; thus this holy calling being prepared from the foundation of the world for such as would not harden their hearts, being in and through the atonement of the Only Begotten Son, who was prepared—"(Alma 13:3-5, BM)

Apparently, we were taught, had our agency, were able to choose good and evil, and exercise faith in our lives before we were born into mortality. This would lead us to the fact that we were able to repent in the pre-earth life as well as learn and grow while we were spirits before we were born.

Notice in verse 4 that some hardened their hearts and rejected the Spirit of God. Revelations talks about a war in heaven where the Devil (Satan) "…was cast out into the earth, and his angels were cast out with him." (Rev 12:7-9) The Doctrine and Covenants sheds a little more light on this stating that Satan rebelled against God "…and also a third part of the hosts of heaven turned he away from me because of their agency." (D&C 29:36) Moses was also taught this truth:

> "Wherefore, because that Satan rebelled against me, and sought to destroy the agency of man, which I, the Lord God, had given him, and also, that I should give unto him mine own power; by the power of mine Only Begotten, I caused that he should be cast down; And he became Satan, yea, even the devil, the father of all lies, to deceive and to blind men, and to lead them captive at his will, even as many as would not hearken unto my voice." (Moses 4:3-4, PGP)

They were not only cast out for hardening their hearts, they were actively trying to destroy our agency, which is one of the greatest gifts God has given each of us. They used their agency and were cast out. We used our agency and get to experience mortality. But we need to be very alert because Satan and his 1/3 of the hosts of heaven are still here trying "to deceive and blind men, and to lead them captive at his will, even as many as [will] not hearken unto my voice." (Moses 4:4, PGP)

If we worked really hard in the first life and were able to become one of the noble and great ones (or even close to it), and then we waste our mortal life chasing after worldly pleasures or letting ourselves get distracted by the noise and activities of the world thus not becoming all that we can be, then when we get to the next life and see where we were in the pre-earth life in progression and our lack of progression in this life—therein lies hell—the regrets, the "should haves," "would haves," or "could haves" of life.

The beauty of it all is that our Heavenly Father and Jesus Christ had the perfect plan from the beginning. Knowing we would be cut off with no memory of our previous lessons, this mortal life became the test. The test to see if we would choose to be good, kind, nice, generous, loving, honest, and helpful (the list could go on) when given choices in the varying circumstances of life. Then if we mess up and choose incorrectly, we have the chance to change and to change completely! This is the safety catch built into the plan.

Satan would have us believe our mistakes are too great, our habits are too engrained. Don't believe him. Remember, Alma was a priest of the wicked king Noah living in sin (Mosiah chapters 11-16). Alma was converted in chapter 17 and went on to become a prophet. Paul (formerly Saul) was murdering the followers of Christ and he became an apostle after his conversion.

Christ's atonement was a gift for all if they would but receive. In his own words: "For behold, I, God, have suffered these things for all, that they might not suffer if they would repent; But if they would not repent they must suffer even as I; Which suffering caused myself, even God, the greatest of all, to tremble because of pain, and to bleed at every pore, and to suffer both body and spirit—and would that I might not drink the bitter cup, and shrink— Nevertheless, glory be to the Father, and I partook and finished my preparations unto the children of men." (D&C 19:16-19)

Always remember,

> "…we are the children of God: And if children, then heirs; heirs of God, and joint-heirs with Christ." (Rom 8:16-17)

> "And the Lord said, who then is that faithful and wise steward, whom his lord shall make ruler over his household,

to give them their portion of meat in due season? Blessed is that servant, whom his Lord when he cometh shall find so doing. Of a truth I say unto you, that he will make him ruler over all that he hath." (Luke 12:42-44)

Joint heirs with Christ…ruler over all that he hath…what grand and glorious things await us if we will only be actively engaged in a good cause. Let us use the Atonement through repentance to become the very best we are capable of, leaving no regrets in the next life. Remember, "…suffering, punishment, confession, remorse, and sorrow may sometimes accompany repentance, but they are not repentance." (August 1988 Ensign, "The Meaning of Repentance") True repentance is actually a change of mind, thought, or thinking so powerful that it changes one's very way of life. We can become "joint-heirs with Christ"! (Rom 8:17)

CHAPTER 4

Why Make and Keep Covenants?

Suppose you were starting a company and had to hire a team to run it. How would you choose your team? What qualities would you want within your team? A few of the important qualities would probably be honesty, integrity, perseverance, willingness to try, obedience, thoughtfulness, ability to make decisions, and the ability to work as a team. The list could probably go on. If this company were to be successful, you would need strength from the top to the bottom and a sense of unity.

God states that His main goal is to "bring to pass the immortality and eternal life of man" (Moses 1:39, PGP). His house is a "house of order" (D&C 123:8). He gives us commandments to test our ability to develop all of the qualities above and more. We experience hardships, relationships, responsibilities, and mortality for the same purpose—to learn, to grow, and to become a successful part of the team. "…God is not interested in His children just becoming trained and obedient 'pets' who will not chew on His slippers in the celestial living room. No, God wants His children to grow up spiritually and join Him in the family business." (Nov 2018 Ensign, Choose you This Day, Elder Dale G Renlund) God gave us commandments with the hope we would choose to obey them, in essence, choose His way.

How well we follow His instructions, use the atonement of Christ to keep changing, and develop ourselves to become the best we are capable of, determines how much responsibility He will entrust us with in the next life. When a person is ready for this kind of development, then they are willing to start making promises with God.

A Covenant is a two-way promise. We promise to do certain things and God promises certain blessings in return. These covenants are entered into formally with Priesthood ordinances. Remember, God's house is a house of order, not one of chaos. All things will be done in an orderly fashion and records will be kept. Once a person formally makes a promise with God and keeps his/her promise, then they are ensured that God will keep His promise. "I, the Lord, am abound when ye do what I say; but when ye do not what I say, ye have no promise." (D&C 82:10) Many years ago, President Boyd K. Packer warned, "Good conduct without the ordinances of the gospel will neither redeem nor exalt mankind." (Boyd K. Packer, "The Only True Church," Ensign, Nov. 1985, 82.)

In <u>True to the Faith</u> we read: "An ordinance is a sacred, formal act performed by the authority of the priesthood. [The] ordinances [that] are essential to our exaltation ... are called saving ordinances. They include baptism, confirmation, ordination to the Melchizedek Priesthood (for men), the temple endowment, and the marriage sealing. (True to the Faith: A Gospel Reference (2004), 109; see also Handbook 2: Administering the Church (2010), 2.1.2.)

I have heard people question the baptism of children as young as eight years old. They claim children that young have no idea what they are doing. The scriptures give us this instruction:

> "Behold I say unto you that this thing shall ye teach—repentance and baptism unto those who are accountable and capable of committing sin; yea, teach parents that they must repent and be baptized, and humble themselves as their little children, and they shall all be saved with their little children." (Moroni 8:10, BM)

> The Doctrine and Covenants further clarifies:
> "And again, inasmuch as parents have children in Zion, or in any of her stakes, which are organized, that teach them not to understand the doctrine of repentance, faith in Christ the Son of the living God, and of baptism and the gift of the Holy Ghost by the laying on of the hands, when eight years old, the sin be upon the heads of the parents. For this shall be a law unto the inhabitants of Zion, or in any of her stakes which are organized. And their children shall be baptized for the remission of their sins when eight years old, and receive the laying on of the hands." (D&C 68:25-27)

God teaches us that if children are taught by their parents, they have sufficient knowledge to make a promise with God to keep His commandments and to always remember Him. Let's not forget that after baptism is the very important ordinance of confirmation with which is given the Gift of the Holy Ghost. If a child is not "capable of committing sin" prior to the age of accountability, then what a gift and a blessing the Gift of the Holy Ghost is when it is given to them at the very time they become accountable for their own actions. The scriptures tell us the Holy Ghost can teach us all things (John 14:26), can bring things to our remembrance (John 14:26), will guide you into all truth (John 16:13), will show you all things what ye should do (2 Nephi 32:5, BM), and will testify to your heart of the divinity of God the Father and Jesus Christ (2 Nephi 31:18, BM). The trick is to help teach them (and learn for ourselves) how to listen, comprehend, and act on the promptings the Holy Ghost gives us.

Taking the Sacrament each Sunday renews those covenants and promises we made to keep His commandments and to always remember Him. At the end of each of the Sacrament prayers (one for the bread and one for the water) the promise given to us for keeping our part of the covenant is "that they may always have his Spirit to be with them." (Moroni 4:3, BM; Moroni 5:2, BM; Doctrine and Covenants 20:77, 79) I have had many experiences in my life that have confirmed this is real.

When I was a sophomore in college, a young man named Steve (name has been changed) was a freshman and a recent convert to The Church of Jesus Christ of Latter-day Saints. He attended the single student ward I attended. I didn't know him very well but knew him enough to say hi and carry on a conversation. One Sunday in early December my roommate and I were singing a musical number in another ward's sacrament meeting before our ward's meetings began. As I was sitting there, the thought came to me to give Steve a Christmas card. I acknowledged the thought and made a mental note to do that. Before the meeting was over, the same thought came again with more force, so I leaned over and told my roommate we needed to stop at the apartment on our way to our ward's meetings.

We stopped at the apartment as planned so I could grab a card and an envelope. In our ward the women's meeting was first. During that meeting's lesson, the thought came again to fill out that card and give it to Steve. So I wrote a message in the card and sealed it in the envelope.

At the end of the meeting, I went in search of Steve. He was in the corner by the door talking to another fellow. I went up to him and gave him the card. He looked at it without opening it. He whispered something to the other fellow and they walked out of the building.

Later I found out Steve had taken an entire bottle of Tylenol the night before to end his life. The only other person that knew about it was the fellow he was talking to. When I handed him the card, he realized someone cared and God knew who he was; he wanted to live. He told his friend and they left for the hospital. Steve survived after a long struggle with his liver trying to shut down.

Sometimes the promptings we get are just a thought (direct and to the point). Or it can come as a feeling. Occasionally an actual voice will be heard. But if we listen and act on those feelings or thoughts, God can direct us to help others or help ourselves.

As we learn, grow, and become more familiar with our covenant of Baptism and the Gift of the Holy Ghost, we can move on, taking on further responsibility by entering into more covenants with our Father in Heaven. Men can progress through taking on the mantle of the Priesthood.

> "God gives priesthood authority to worthy male members of the Church [of Jesus Christ of Latter-day Saints] so they can act in His name for the salvation of His children.... Although the authority of the priesthood is bestowed only on worthy male members of the Church [of Jesus Christ of Latter-day Saints], the blessings of the priesthood are available to all—men, women, and children. We all benefit from the influence of righteous priesthood leadership, and we all have the privilege of receiving the saving ordinances of the priesthood."
> (True to the Faith: A Gospel Reference (2004), 124)

Then further growth and strength can be obtained through temple ordinances and covenants. Ultimately families can be sealed together for time and all eternity! All of these ordinances are connected to covenants. To grow to our full potential, we need to work at keeping our promises to God. We need to continue to grow and develop to become the strongest team player we have the capability of becoming. If we do all in our power, then Christ's atonement will pick up any slack our mortality may have dealt us including our mistakes, frailties, and weaknesses. We must also remember that we are all in this together. We need to love and support one another on this journey. To judge, belittle, antagonize, or ostracize one another would be counterproductive to strengthening the team.

Making formal covenants (two-way promises) with God through Priesthood ordinances that are recorded both in Heaven and on Earth, puts us on the covenant path that will make us stronger and ready to take on assignments in God's Kingdom here on earth and beyond. We become a strong team player.

CHAPTER 5

Why Temples?

God and Jesus Christ teach differently than mortal human beings do. They teach in a fashion that those who are ready to learn more can learn more; those that are only ready for the basics can get the basics, all from the same story or lesson. Jesus's parables and teachings during His mortal life are very good examples of this. So are the temple ordinances.

Temple ordinances (covenants) and teachings are sacred, and the things learned there can be applied to our lives and develop our eternal perspective. We go to the temple the first time to make covenants with our Heavenly Father for ourselves. We can continue to go to the temple and make those same covenants for our ancestors who didn't have the chance in mortality. The repetition, for us, allows us to continue to learn more ourselves and gain that deeper understanding. For our ancestors it gives them the option to accept or reject those same covenants.

In 1 Peter it tells of Christ suffering for sins and "being put to death in the flesh, but quickened by the Spirit: By which also he went and preached unto the spirits in prison; which sometime were disobedient," (1 Peter 3:18-20) "For for this cause was the gospel preached also to them that are dead, that they might be judged according to men in the flesh, but live according to God in the spirit." (1 Peter 4:6) John witnessed this also. In John 5:25 he states: "…the dead shall hear the voice of the Son of God: and they that hear shall live." Paul posed the following question to the Corinthians; "…what shall they do which are baptized for the dead, if the dead rise not at all? Why are they then baptized for the dead?" (1 Corinthians 15:29) Apparently, they were doing baptisms by proxy for the dead after Christ's crucifixion. Today we can be baptized by proxy for our ancestors in the temples of The Church of Jesus Christ of Latter-day Saints.

One must conclude, after reading Peter's, John's, and Paul's writings, that our ancestors are taught after they leave this life and can choose to receive these covenants or reject them. We do the service of proxy ordinances for them so they have the opportunity to progress if they so desire. These ordinances are only performed in temples of The Church of Jesus Christ of Latter-day Saints dedicated by Priesthood authority for doing the work of the Lord.

In 1918 President Joseph F. Smith, while contemplating the above New Testament scriptures, was taught that Christ's

> "…ministry among those who were dead was limited to the brief time intervening between the crucifixion and his resurrection; …and I perceived that the Lord went not in person among the wicked and the disobedient who had rejected the truth, to teach them; But behold, from among the righteous, he organized his forces and appointed messengers,…" (D&C 138:27, 29)

> " I beheld that the faithful elders of this dispensation, when they depart from mortal life, continue their labors in the preaching of the gospel of repentance and redemption, through the sacrifice of the Only Begotten Son of God, among those who are in darkness and under the bondage of sin in the great world of the spirits of the dead. The dead who repent will be redeemed, through obedience to the ordinances of the house of God, And after they have paid the penalty of their transgressions, and are washed clean, shall receive a reward according to their works, for they are heirs of salvation." (D&C 138: 57-59)

In order to be "redeemed, through obedience to the ordinances of the house of God," they have to receive the ordinances of the house of God. I've heard some people say, "I don't have to be righteous and go to the temple because you will do it for me when I die." Please note in verse 59 the words "after they have paid the penalty of their transgressions." This takes us back to repentance. In Doctrine & Covenants section 19:15-19 Christ explains:

> "Therefore I command you to repent—repent, lest I smite you by the rod of my mouth, and by my wrath, and by my

anger, and your sufferings be sore—how sore you know not, how exquisite you know not, yea, how hard to bear you know not. For behold, I, God, have suffered these things for all, that they might not suffer if they would repent; But if they would not repent they must suffer even as I; Which suffering caused myself, even God, the greatest of all, to tremble because of pain, and to bleed at every pore, and to suffer both body and spirit—and would that I might not drink the bitter cup, and shrink—Nevertheless, glory be to the Father, and I partook and finished my preparations unto the children of men."

If we take advantage of Christ's atonement while here in mortality, He did the suffering part for us.

While teaching seminary I heard of a hands-on lesson and decided to try the lesson in my classroom to see if I would get the same results. (http://devanjensen.blogspot.com/2012/04/parable-of-push-ups.html?q=the+parable+of+the+push-ups) I asked a young man in the class that was physically fit if he thought he could do 200 pushups in sets of 10 (let's call him Troy). (We had twenty or twenty-two students in the class). He was pretty confident he could. So I bought a bunch of candy bars (the original story I read used donuts). The day of the lesson, I started at one side of the class and asked the first person if they would like a candy bar. Of course the answer was yes, so I asked Troy if he would do ten pushups so they could have a candy bar. He jumped down and did ten pushups. By person number four or five they no longer wanted the candy bar. I asked Troy to do ten pushups so "Jill" could have a candy bar she didn't want. He did. The boys were starting to say they would do their own pushups, but that wasn't allowed. Troy did pushups so the boys who didn't want a candy bar could have one. By about the seventeenth person a couple more students showed up late. The other kids told them not to come in. I asked Troy if it was okay if they came in. He cheerfully said yes from his place on the floor (by this time it was too much effort to get up and down each time). Some of the girls were in tears. Troy succeeded and did ten pushups for every person in the class to get a candy bar. Then we read the scriptures above where Christ describes His own suffering.

If the students felt bad enough to have tears for Troy doing pushups so they could have a candy bar, multiply that by billions or more people that Christ suffered for, to atone not only for all of mankind's sins, but our sufferings, injustices, illnesses, and sorrows. Christ has already paid the price for us to change and repent without having to suffer ourselves. All we have to do is take advantage of the time we have in this life to become the best team player for God's Kingdom that we have the capability of becoming. This includes making and keeping sacred covenants with God and using the power of the atonement throughout our lives.

The crowning temple ordinance is that of sealing families together for all eternity. No longer do we have to live with the fear of death causing a permanent separation from our spouses or families. This, too, is part of God's house of order and unity. Families can be together forever but these connections are not only saved for the next life.

When I was in college, spring of 1986, I had two roommates. One was from Cokeville, Wyoming, USA and the other had grandparents that lived in Cokeville. This town was predominantly made up of members of The Church of Jesus Christ of Latter-day Saints. That spring a deranged couple took the Cokeville Elementary School hostage with guns and a homemade bomb. They had the student population and teachers all in one classroom. (This event was later made into a movie The Cokeville Miracle, Christianbook.com.) My roommates were glued to the television and beside themselves with fear. The three of us knelt down and said a prayer for them. The bomb went off accidentally but not a single student or teacher died. A few ended up in the burn ward in a Utah hospital, but all recovered.

About a week later stories started coming back through my roommate who had cousins in the school. One small girl was at her grandmother's house admiring the family pictures on the back of the piano. She told her grandma that she knew "that lady." Her grandma told her she couldn't know "that lady" because she died before the girl was born. The girl simply replied, "But she is the one that helped me out the window when the bomb went off."

Our families can be there for us on both sides of the veil. We can help give them the ordinances they need to progress and grow; they can help us when we need them. The ties are eternal.

Temples are very important in the organization of God's "house." To find those willing to put in the effort to become strong team players, he not only gives us commandments to follow but he wants us to put some skin in the game by making promises with Him (some of these in temples) and following through. Would you expect any less from your team players?

CHAPTER 6

Why Prayer?

When a child asks a question, or asks for something they want or need, a good parent will respond to the request. If it is good for the child, they will receive what they asked for. If it is not good for the child, the answer will be no or not now.

> "If ye then being evil, know how to give good gifts unto your children, how much more shall your Father which is in heaven give good things to them that ask him?" (Matthew 7:11)

The key is to recognize we have a loving Father in Heaven that has our best interest in mind and is willing to help us.

> "As soon as we learn the true relationship in which we stand toward God (namely, God is our Father, and we are His children), then at once prayer becomes natural and instinctive on our part." (Bible Dictionary, 'Prayer')

Our "Father knoweth what things ye have need of, before ye ask him" (Matthew 6:8) so why ask? God gave us our agency.

- "...choose...whom ye will serve" (Joshua 24:15)
- "...men are free...to choose" (2 Nephi 2:27, BM)
- "...gave I unto man his agency" (Moses 7:32, PGP)

If God gave us agency and expects us to choose, He will not interfere unless asked to.

When my family was young, with all six children at home, we were gathering for lunch one summer day. We prayed at each meal and it happened to be my turn to pray that day. My husband and a couple of neighbors were working to build a shop and were late for lunch. As I started to pray, I had a strong impression to pray for the safety of the men building the shop. I did. A few minutes later my husband brought one of the neighbors in with a severely broken nose. A thick walled three- or four-inch metal pipe about fifteen feet long, that was being used as a support, let loose and silently fell on our neighbor's face. If it would have been a fraction of an inch to the side it would have hit his temple and probably killed him. As it was, it barely missed his tear duct saving his eye from future damage. God wants us to ask and won't interfere unless we do. I was prompted to ask so He could help.

The scriptures list many blessings that await those that pray. One of the biggest is to ask with faith and ye shall receive. This is repeated many times throughout the scriptures with a little variance in wording. (Matthew 7:7, Matthew 21:22; Mark 11:24; 3 Nephi 14:7, BM; 3 Nephi 18:20, BM; Moroni 7:26, BM; Doctrine and Covenants 4:7, 6:5, 66:9) Some of the other blessings promised or received as the result of prayer are:

- "Pray always, and I will pour out my Spirit upon you, and great shall be your blessing—yea, even more than if you should obtain treasures of earth…" (Doctrine and Covenants 19:38)

- "…shall be delivered…" (Joel 2:32)

- Escape calamities preceding the second coming (Luke 21:36)

- "…that ye may not be tempted above that which ye can bear, and thus be led by the Holy Spirit, becoming humble, meek, submissive, patient, full of love and all long-suffering." (Alma 13:28, BM)

- "…pray one for another that ye may be healed. The effectual fervent prayer of a righteous man availeth much." (James 5:16)

- "If any of you lack wisdom, let him ask of God, that giveth to all men liberally, and upbraideth not; and it shall be given him." (James 1:5)

- "…calling upon God, he received strength…" (Moses 1:20, PGP)

God does add a few stipulations if followed will make our prayers more effective:

- "But let him ask in faith, nothing wavering. For he that

- wavereth is like a wave of the sea driven with the wind and tossed." (James 1:6)
- "…use not vain repetitions…" (Matthew 6:7)
- "…charity is the pure love of Christ…pray unto the Father with all the energy of heart, that ye may be filled with this love…" (Moroni 7:47-48, BM)
- "…do all in the name of the Lord Jesus, giving thanks to God and the Father by him." (Colossians 3:17)
- "…you must study it out in your mind; then you must ask me if it be right, and if it is right, I will cause that your bosom shall burn within you; therefore, you shall feel that it is right." (Doctrine and Covenants 9:8)

He also warns us to ask for what is right.

- "Ye ask, and receive not, because ye ask amiss" (James 4:3)
- "…I know that God will give liberally to him that asketh. Yea, my God will give me, if I ask not amiss…" (2 Nephi 4:35, BM)
- "…do not ask for that which you ought not." (Doctrine and Covenants 8:10)

I have learned that if you are unsure of what is right to ask for in your prayers, pray and ask God what is most important to ask for. Then listen. When I did this, the thoughts that came into my mind were not my own. Those things brought to my mind weren't even on my radar screen, but they were the most important things I should be praying for.

Sometimes it is hard to determine whether your prayers are being heard. One time not so long ago, I was experiencing a really stressful time in life. We were experiencing tight finances. My husband was living and working in one state, with myself and the kids living two states away for them to be in school. I was feeling like evil was trying really hard to enter our home. I had been praying for some specific things:

- That our cars would continue to run since we didn't have the ability to replace them.
- That we would be able to keep evil out of our home.
- That my husband would be safe and have the spirit to guide him.

- That my children would have the spirit to be with them and give them a desire to grow closer to the Lord.

At this time, I was assigned new home teachers. One day, one of them and his wife, (new to our ward) stopped by and asked if we needed anything. I told him that with my husband away a lot we may need to call on him for priesthood blessings if needed. He agreed.

A couple of Sundays later, he stopped me in church and asked if he could visit us that night. During his visit he offered to give me a blessing. I accepted. Then he asked if there was anything in particular I needed. I told him whatever the spirit dictates. The blessing contained everything I had been praying for! I knew my prayers were being heard and my home teacher had been sent to give me that message.

> "Prayer is the act by which the will of the Father and the will of the child are brought into correspondence with each other. The object of prayer is not to change the will of God but to secure for ourselves and for others blessings that God is already willing to grant but that are made conditional on our asking for them. Blessings require some work or effort on our part before we can obtain them. Prayer is a form of work and is an appointed means for obtaining the highest of all blessings." (Bible Dictionary, "Prayer")

> "We pray in Christ's name when our mind is the mind of Christ, and our wishes the wishes of Christ—when His words abide in us (John 15:7). We then ask for things it is possible for God to grant. Many prayers remain unanswered because they are not in Christ's name at all; they in no way represent His mind but spring out of the selfishness of man's heart." (Bible Dictionary, "Prayer")

Prayer is our "cell phone" to God. Luckily, the thing that powers it is the desires of our heart. May we keep those desires pure and focused so we can strengthen that connection and obtain the desired knowledge, blessings, and help we need.

CHAPTER 7

Why Sabbath Day Observance?

God was very clear when he gave Moses the 10 commandments. He said:

> "Remember the Sabbath day, to keep it holy. Six days shalt thou labour, and do all thy work: But the seventh day is the Sabbath of the LORD thy God: in it thou shalt not do any work, thou, nor thy son, nor thy daughter, thy manservant, nor thy maidservant, nor thy cattle, nor thy stranger that is within thy gates: For in six days the LORD made heaven and earth, the sea, and all that in them is, and rested the seventh day: wherefore the LORD blessed the Sabbath day, and hallowed it." (Exodus 20: 8-11)

Later in Leviticus the Lord gives more details of promised blessings for keeping this commandment, and promised scourges or problems if a people fail to keep it.

> "Ye shall keep my Sabbaths…If ye walk in my statues, and keep my commandments… Then I will give you rain in due season, and the land shall yield her increase, and the trees of the field shall yield their fruit… and ye shall eat your bread to the full, and dwell in your land safely. And I will give peace in the land, and ye shall lie down, and none shall make you afraid… neither shall the sword go through your land." (Leviticus 26:2-6)

"But if ye will not hearken unto me, and will not do all these commandments; And if ye shall despise my statutes, or if your soul abhor my judgments, so that ye will not do all my commandments, but that ye break my covenant: I also will do this unto you; ... terror, consumption, and the burning ague, that shall consume the eyes, and cause sorrow of heart: and ye shall sow your seed in vain, for your enemies shall eat it... .ye shall be slain before your enemies: they that hate you shall reign over you; ... your land shall not yield her increase,... plagues...wild beasts... shall rob you of your children, and destroy your cattle, and make you few in number; and your highways shall be desolate. ...I will bring a sword upon you ... I will send the pestilence among you; and ye shall be delivered into the hand of the enemy." (Leviticus 26:14-25)

Two very different pictures. And we get to pick which picture we want to bring upon ourselves, our families, our communities, and our countries. Our modern-day prophets and apostles have been warning and urging us very strongly for the last decade to keep the Sabbath day holy. The world is full of war, and with the tensions of the world increasing dramatically. Wouldn't we be wise to make a few simple changes in our lifestyles so the Lord will be on our side, and in our camp when the relative peace we have enjoyed starts to unravel. Just think, if an entire nation kept the Sabbath day holy, it would decrease the potential of war on that land.

That brings us to the question of what changes in our lifestyles do we need to make? Each of us has to answer that question for ourselves, but we find some directives in the Doctrine and Covenants section 59:

- ...thou shalt go to the house of prayer and offer up thy sacraments upon my holy day (vs. 9)
- ...rest from your labors (vs. 10)
- ...offer thine oblations [time, talents, or means, in the service of God and fellowmen (footnote b, vs. 12)] (vs. 12)
- ...on this day thou shalt do none other thing, only let thy food be prepared with singleness of heart that thy fasting [hungering and thirsting after righteousness (footnote a, vs. 13)] may be perfect, or, in other words, that thy joy may be full. (vs. 13)

- ...do these things with thanksgiving, with cheerful hearts and countenances (vs. 15)

This section also lists many additional blessings we can obtain by being obedient to this commandment:

- ...that thou mayest more fully keep thyself unspotted from the world (vs. 9)
- ...the fullness of the earth is yours (vs. 16)
- ...peace in this world and eternal life in the world to come (vs. 23)

Thus, taking a day off from our normal routine, serving our fellowman, taking time to reflect on the things of eternity and learn more about them, will give us all the blessings and promises that God wishes to bestow upon us. Life is hard enough with all of its challenges. If each of us individually and in combination, our society as a whole, were to keep this basic commandment faithfully, think of the changes we could bring about to help ease those challenges, even if only by a little bit. God keeps his promises; all He asks is obedience.

CHAPTER 8

Why Perfection?
(Can I be perfect?)

Before his crucifixion and subsequent resurrection, Christ taught his disciples, "Be ye therefore perfect, even as your Father which is in heaven is perfect." (Matthew 5:48) After His resurrection he taught the Nephites on the American continent, "...be perfect even as I, or your Father who is in heaven is perfect." (3 Nephi 12:48, BM) Note that before His resurrection Christ only denotes the Father as being perfect. After his resurrection He includes himself. This teaches us that Christ was not perfected until after the resurrection.

What does it mean to be perfect? Is it really attainable? President Russell M. Nelson taught:

> "The term perfect was translated from the Greek teleios, which means 'complete' ...The infinitive form of the verb is teleiono, which means 'to reach a distant end, to be fully developed, to consummate, or to finish.' Please note that the word does not imply 'freedom from error'; it implies 'achieving a distant objective'...The Lord taught, 'Ye are not able to abide the presence of God now...; wherefore, continue in patience until ye are perfected' (D&C 67:13)" ("Perfection Pending," Ensign, Nov. 1995, 86, 88)

In the New Testament Peter gives us a pretty basic list of things to work on so we can become "complete" or "fully developed" as "partakers of the divine nature."

> "...that by these ye might be partakers of the divine nature, having escaped the corruption that is in the world... faith... virtue... knowledge... temperance... patience... godliness... brotherly kindness... charity.... For if these things be in you, and abound, they make you that ye shall neither be barren nor unfruitful in the knowledge of our Lord Jesus Christ." (2 Peter 1:4-8)

The key word to all of this is BECOME. We don't have to do it all today. Every day of our lives is an opportunity to improve on the days that went before. All we have to do is try to do better each day and keep the commandments. The promises that come with this are huge!

> "...come unto Christ, and be perfected in him, and deny yourselves of all ungodliness; and if ye shall deny yourselves of all ungodliness and love God with all your might, mind, and strength, then is his grace sufficient for you, that by his grace ye may be perfect in Christ;" (Moroni 10:32, BM)

> "To him that overcometh will I grant to sit with me in my throne, even as I also overcame, and am set down with my Father in his throne." (Revelations 3:21)

Obedience and practice are key. If we want to improve our abilities at anything we have to practice. I am a musician. I may have a genetic tendency towards music, or it may be a "memory" of something I learned in the pre-earth life, but I still had to practice for years to develop the ability to play instruments and sing. It is in our spiritual DNA to be "joint-heirs with Christ" (Romans 8:17). Just like a talent or skill it will not be handed to us. We must want it enough to study it out and practice to achieve it. Otherwise it will simply be an unsatisfied desire and possibly one of life's regrets.

"We need not be dismayed if our earnest efforts toward perfection now seem so arduous and endless. Perfection is pending. It can come in full only after the Resurrection and only through the Lord. It awaits all who love him and keep his commandments." (Russell M. Nelson, "Perfection Pending," Ensign, Nov. 1995, 86, 88)

AFTERWORD:

My Testimony

I know God lives and He is our literal Father in Heaven. I know Jesus Christ was born of a virgin, lived his life as recorded in the New Testament, suffered in Gethsemane for all of humankind, died on the Cross only to rise a resurrected being three days later as directed by God our Father. I know God hears and answers our prayers and that his plan for us extends far beyond this mortal life we are experiencing right now. I know all of this because as I study and learn, the Spirit (Holy Ghost) communicates and confirms the truths I learn. One cannot learn eternal truths and make the deeper connections without the Spirit's guidance. If you close your mind and heart to His influence, you close your mind and heart to a whole new realm of knowledge.

My prayer is that you will find in your hearts a greater desire to learn eternal truths that you can carry with you after this life is over. Knowledge is the one thing we get to take with us into the next stage of our existence. What a joy it will be to have some of the knowledge of the eternal realm when we get there so we don't have to start from square one.

CPSIA information can be obtained
at www.ICGtesting.com
Printed in the USA
BVHW010911280521
607999BV00021B/970